pickles & chutneys

THE AUSTRALIAN
Women's Weekly

Pickling and preserving are time-honoured ways of offering vegetables out of season. Now that we have so many vegetables available in our shops throughout the year, there is really no reason not to make the very most of them. Whether you choose to pickle some crisp onions or caramelise your vegetables into a chutney, you will be amazed at just how easy it can be. Friends and family will love a carefully labelled bottle from you for Christmas with its own unique message!

Pamela Clark

Food Director

contents

tips & techniques

Here are some tried-and-tested tips that will give you success every time; they are simple techniques that work perfectly, and it's important to read them before you start to cook. If you follow these procedures, your pickles, chutneys and sauces will be a triumph – tasty, delicious and simple to prepare.

CHUTNEYS, PICKLES, RELISHES AND SAUCES

These are all condiments made from vegetables, fruits, sugar, spices and vinegar. With these preserves, it is often necessary to secure whole spices in a muslin bag to be cooked with the preserve. This bag is discarded later.

chutneys

A condiment of Indian origin, chutney is a kind of tangy sweet pickle usually served as an accompaniment to hot and cold meats, cheese and savouries. A little can make a sandwich sublime or give oomph to cold meat or a grilled chop. Mango chutney is a classic accompaniment

to curries. There are many varieties, all based on chopped fruit and/or vegetables, sugar and vinegar. Not much can go wrong as mixtures are simply cooked until thick. Once you have opened a jar, keep, covered, in the fridge.

pickles
Pickles mainly fall into two categories: those that have a clear, sweet and/or spicy vinegar poured over various vegetables, or those that are thick and pulpy. These are thickened either by slow cooking to evaporate the liquid and concentrate the flavours, or by thickening the liquid with flour. Generally, you need wide-mouthed jars for the vinegar-based recipes, and vegetables are chopped to suit your own taste. In these cases, we haven't specified the quantities the pickles will make as it depends on the chopped size and how tightly the vegetables are packed into the jars. It is vital that the ingredients are completely covered with the vinegar mixture to complete the pickling process and to prevent the vegetables from deteriorating. All pickles should be refrigerated after opening.

relishes
Sharp, tangy relishes are based on fruit and/or vegetables and usually contain sugar and vinegar, but generally not in large enough

Microwave cooking

The flavour and colour of microwave cooked preserves is excellent. The golden rule is keep checking the preserve as it cooks.
- Always use a large shallow container, cook, covered or uncovered as the recipes state, check constantly during the cooking time.
- **Chutneys and pickles** can be cooked in small quantities in a microwave oven but, as evaporation is a necessary part of the cooking process, it is best to cook these preserves in the conventional way.
- **Relishes** are usually fine to microwave; the colour retention is excellent.

quantities to preserve the ingredients for as long as most other pickles. Relishes must be stored in the fridge and will keep for about a month. They add zest to hot or cold meats, curries and savoury snacks.

sauces

The beauty of home made sauces is that they can be as thick or as thin as you like. Simply cook the mixture until it's about the consistency you want, let a tablespoon of the mixture cool to room temperature. Test the consistency again and cook further if not thick enough. The sauce recipes in this book should be kept in the fridge after they have been opened.

EQUIPMENT

When making preserves, use large, wide-topped saucepans or boilers made of either aluminium (providing the preserve is not left standing in the pan for more than an hour), stainless steel or enamel. Never use copper or unsealed cast-iron pans; the acid in the preserve will damage the metal, and colour and flavour ingredients.

INGREDIENTS

vinegar Use a good-quality malt vinegar; cheap vinegars do not contain enough acetic acid to act as a preservative. Good vinegar contains at least 4 per cent acetic acid.

salt We have used minimal salt in our recipes. Taste the preserve before bottling; add salt to suit your taste.

sugar This, along with vinegar, is the ingredient that preserves these home-cooked products. The only difference is in the colour and how that colour affects the finished preserve.

• Brown and white sugars are used in chutneys, pickles, relishes, sauces, etc. Brown or black sugar simply gives a richer colour and flavour.

• To warm sugar, spread sugar into a baking dish, it should not be more than about 3cm deep. Place dish into slow oven for about 10 minutes, stir the sugar occasionally to distribute the warmth evenly.

fruit and vegetables The fruit and vegetables used for preserving must be unblemished and well washed.

• **berries and currants** Freshly picked, slightly under-ripe perfect fruit is always the best; however, frozen fruit can be substituted. If you don't have scales it is handy to know that 250g berries will fill a 250ml measuring cup or jug.

• **apples** We used Granny Smith apples throughout this book. Try to obtain apples which are as freshly picked as possible and preferably under-ripe. Apples which have been in cold storage will not give such good results.

Jars & bottles

Jars and bottles must be glass, without chips or cracks; and should be sterilised. As a general rule, hot preserves go into hot sterilised jars, cold preserves go into cold sterilised jars. Jars must always be dry. Tea-towels and hands must be clean when handling jars. Unclean jars can cause deterioration in preserves.

To sterilise jars
in dishwasher: use rinse cycle and hottest temperature, do not use detergent.
without a dishwasher: method 1: place clean jars lying down in pan, cover completely with cold water, cover pan, bring to boil and boil, covered, for 20 minutes; carefully remove jars from water (thick rubber gloves and tongs are useful for this); drain well, stand right way up on wooden board. The heat from the jars will quickly evaporate any water remaining in the jars. method 2: wash jars well in hot soapy water, rinse thoroughly in hot water. Stand jars right way up on board in cold oven (do not allow jars to touch); turn oven to very low, leave for 30 minutes, remove from oven.

To seal jars
Preserve must be correctly sealed while it is still hot in order to prevent deterioration. Ordinary metal lids are not suitable; the acid content of the preserve will corrode the lids and the contents will be inedible. Special lined and treated or lacquered lids are suitable for sealing. Plastic screw-top lids give a good seal (plastic snap-on lids are not airtight enough). Plastic lids must be well washed, rinsed and dried. Some older preserving jars have glass lids; these can be sterilised by either of the above methods. Do not use aluminium foil, cellophane or paper covers for preserves; foil will be corroded by the acid in the preserves and paper and cellophane are not airtight enough for long term keeping. Wipe sealed jars clean, label and date.

To store jars
Store preserves in a cool, airy, dark, dry place (light can cause deterioration) until required. Once opened, all preserves must be stored, covered, in the refrigerator.

sweet fruit chutney

1kg apples, peeled, chopped
1kg tomatoes, peeled, chopped
500kg onions, chopped
240g sultanas
120g chopped raisins
150g currants

1 litre malt vinegar
1kg brown sugar
2 teaspoons grated orange rind
2 teaspoons grated fresh ginger
½ teaspoon ground cloves
2 teaspoons ground cinnamon
pinch cayenne pepper

1 Combine all ingredients in large saucepan.
2 Stir over heat, without boiling, until sugar is dissolved. Bring to boil; simmer, uncovered, stirring occasionally, for 1½ hours, or until mixture is thick.
3 Spoon hot chutney into hot sterilised jars; seal while hot.

makes about 1.5 litres

apricot & orange chutney

500g dried apricots
1 litre water
310ml white vinegar
120g sultanas
1 clove garlic crushed
1 tablespoon grated orange rind
80ml orange juice
3 black peppercorns
220g sugar

1   Combine apricots, water, vinegar, sultanas, garlic, rind, juice and
peppercorns in large saucepan. Bring to boil, simmer, covered, for
30 minutes, or until apricots are pulpy. Add sugar, stir over heat, without
boiling, until sugar is dissolved. Bring to boil, simmer, uncovered, for 5 minutes
2   Pour into hot sterilised jars; seal while hot.

makes 1 litre

blackberry & apple chutney

2 large apples (400g), peeled, chopped
2 medium onions (240g), chopped
1kg blackberries
330g brown sugar
500ml malt vinegar
½ teaspoon ground allspice
½ teaspoon ground ginger

1   Combine all ingredients in large saucepan. Stir over heat, without boiling,
until sugar is dissolved. Bring to boil, simmer, uncovered, stirring occasionally,
for 1½ hours, or until mixture is thick.
2   Pour chutney into hot sterilised jars; seal while hot.

makes about 750ml

country garden chutney

1.5kg plums, pitted, chopped
600g apples, peeled, chopped
1kg tomatoes, peeled chopped
500g onions, chopped
280g cucumber, chopped
2 litres malt vinegar
440g brown sugar, firmly packed
1½ tablespoons white mustard seeds
2 teaspoons mixed spice
6 black peppercorns
6 cloves
3 small fresh red chillies
2cm piece fresh ginger, peeled

1 Combine plums, apples, tomatoes, onions, cucumber, vinegar, sugar, seeds and spice in large saucepan.
2 Tie peppercorns, cloves, chillies and ginger in piece of muslin; add to pan. Bring to boil, simmer, uncovered, stirring occasionally, for 1½ hours or until mixture is thick. Discard bag.
3 Pour hot chutney into hot sterilised jars; seal while hot.

makes about 2.5 litres

rhubarb chutney

1kg rhubarb chopped
240g onions chopped
660g brown sugar
240g sultanas
625ml white vinegar

1 tablespoon white mustard
  seeds
1 teaspoon mixed spice
1 teaspoon ground ginger

1 Combine all ingredients in large saucepan. Bring to boil, simmer, uncovered, for 1¼ hours, stirring occasionally, or until mixture is thick.
2 Pour hot chutney into hot sterilised jars; seal while hot.

makes 1.25 litres

apple & date chutney

500ml malt vinegar
220g brown sugar, firmly packed
1 tablespoon grated fresh ginger
2 small fresh red chillies, chopped
1 teaspoon white mustard seeds
500ml water
600g apples
320g pitted dates, chopped
340g raisins, chopped
240g onions, chopped

1 Combine vinegar, sugar, ginger, chillies, seeds and water in large saucepan. Stir over heat, without boiling, until sugar is dissolved. Stir in apples, dates, raisins and onions.
2 Bring to boil, simmer, uncovered, for 1 hour, stirring occasionally or until mixture is thick.
3 Pour hot chutney into hot sterilised jars; seal while hot.

makes about 1.5 litres

apple & prune chutney

1kg apples, peeled, chopped
300g prunes, pitted, chopped
60ml lemon juice
165g sugar
½ teaspoon white vinegar

1 Combine all ingredients in large saucepan, stir over heat until sugar is dissolved. Bring to boil; simmer, uncovered, stirring occasionally, for 30 minutes or until mixture is thick.
2 Pour hot chutney into hot sterilised jars; seal while hot.

makes about 750ml

chutneys & jams

spiced plum chutney

1kg plums, pitted, chopped
5 medium tomatoes (500g), peeled, chopped
3 medium onions (360g), chopped
3 medium carrots (360g), chopped
1 large apple (200g), peeled, chopped
160g chopped raisins
440g brown sugar
2 teaspoons coarse cooking salt
875ml malt vinegar
1 cinnamon stick
½ teaspoon cloves
3 small dried red chillies
1 star anise
1 teaspoon black peppercorns

1 Combine plums, tomatoes, onions, carrots, apples, raisins, sugar, salt and vinegar in large saucepan; stir over heat until sugar is dissolved. Tie cinnamon, cloves, chillies, star anise and peppercorns in piece of muslin. Add muslin bag to pan.
2 Bring to boil; simmer, uncovered, stirring occasionally, for 2 hours or until mixture is thick. Discard muslin bag.
3 Pour hot chutney into hot sterilised jars; seal while hot.

makes about 2.25 litres

peach & raisin chutney

3 medium peaches (450g)
110g finely chopped raisins
125ml cider vinegar
2 tablespoons lemon juice

1 small onion (80g), chopped finely
¼ teaspoon ground cinnamon
½ teaspoon ground allspice
220g white sugar

1 Cover peaches with boiling water in medium heatproof bowl for about 30 seconds. Peel, remove stones, then chop peaches finely.
2 Place in medium saucepan with remaining ingredients; bring to a boil. Reduce heat, simmer, uncovered, stirring occasionally, about 45 minutes or until chutney thickens.
3 Pour hot chutney into hot sterilised jars; seal while hot.

makes about 500ml

plum chutney

60g butter
2 cloves garlic, crushed
2 teaspoons grated fresh ginger
2 teaspoons ground cumin
1 teaspoon ground cardamom
2 teaspoons yellow mustard seeds
2 medium onions (300g), sliced

1kg plums, pitted, chopped
2 large apples (400g), peeled,
   chopped
440g brown sugar
250ml dry red wine
500ml white vinegar

1 Heat butter in large saucepan, add garlic and ginger, cook 1 minute. Stir in spices, seeds and onion; cook until onion is soft. Stir in remaining ingredients, stir over heat, without boiling, until sugar is dissolved.
2 Bring to a boil; simmer, uncovered, stirring occasionally, for about 1½ hours or until thick.
3 Pour hot chutney into hot sterilised jars; seal while hot.

makes about 1.5 litres

peach & cardamom chutney

7 large peaches (1.5kg)
1 large onion (200g), chopped finely
120g coarsely chopped raisins
330g brown sugar
180ml cider vinegar
1 cinnamon stick
4 cardamom pods, bruised
1 teaspoon whole allspice
2 teaspoons finely grated lemon rind

1 Cut small cross in bottom of each peach. Lower gently into large saucepan of boiling water, boil for 1 minute, then place in large bowl of cold water. Peel peaches, remove stones, chop peaches coarsely.
2 Combine peaches with remaining ingredients in large saucepan; stir over heat until sugar dissolves. Bring to the boil; reduce heat. Simmer, uncovered, stirring occasionally, about 45 minutes or until thick.
3 Pour chutney into hot sterilised jars; seal while hot.

makes about 2 litres

banana & date chutney

7 medium bananas (1kg)
500g dates, stones removed, chopped
1 teaspoon grated fresh ginger
1 medium onion (120g), chopped
2 teaspoons grated lemon rind
60ml lemon juice
440g malt vinegar
220g brown sugar
2 teaspoons curry powder

1 Combine bananas, dates, ginger, onion, rind, juice and vinegar in large saucepan. Bring to boil, simmer, uncovered, for about 20 minutes or until fruit is soft. Stir in sugar and curry powder, stir over heat, without boiling, until sugar is dissolved.
2 Bring to boil, simmer, uncovered, stirring occasionally, for about 20 minutes or until mixture is thick.
3 Pour chutney into hot sterilised jars; seal while hot.

makes about 1.25ml

chutneys & jams

pineapple chutney

1 large pineapple (1.5kg), chopped
1 medium onion (120g), chopped
250ml cider vinegar
220g brown sugar, firmly packed
½ teaspoon grated fresh ginger
½ teaspoon chilli powder
¼ teaspoon ground cloves
125ml dry sherry

1 Combine pineapple, onion, vinegar, sugar, ginger, chilli powder and cloves in large saucepan. Stir over heat, without boiling, until sugar is dissolved. Bring to boil, simmer, uncovered, stirring occasionally, for about 20 minutes or until mixture is thick. Stir in sherry.
2 Pour chutney into hot sterilised jars; seal while hot.

makes about 750ml

cherry chutney

1kg cherries, pitted, chopped
150g currants
110g brown sugar
2 tablespoons golden syrup
250ml white vinegar
1¼ teaspoons ground allspice

1 Combine all ingredients in large saucepan. Stir over heat, without boiling, until sugar is dissolved. Bring to boil, simmer, uncovered, stirring occasionally, for about 30 minutes, or until mixture is thick.
2 Pour chutney into hot sterilised jars; seal while hot.

makes about 750ml

green mango chutney

6 green mangoes (2kg), peeled, chopped coarsely
1 tablespoon coarse cooking salt
385g white sugar
625ml malt vinegar
8cm piece ginger (40g), grated
2 cloves garlic, crushed
110g coarsely chopped dates
120g chopped raisins
1 teaspoon chilli powder
1 teaspoon ground cinnamon
1 teaspoon ground cumin

1 Place mangoes and salt in large bowl. Barely cover with cold water, cover; stand overnight. Drain mangoes; discard water.
2 Stir sugar and vinegar in large saucepan over heat, without boiling, until sugar dissolves. Stir in mangoes and remaining ingredients; bring to boil, simmer, uncovered, stirring occasionally, for 45 minutes or until mixture is thick.
3 Spoon hot chutney into hot sterilised jars; seal while hot.

makes about 2 litres

indian chutney

2 large apples (400g), peeled, chopped
4 medium onions (500g), chopped
500g dates, chopped
1 teaspoon cayenne pepper
1 teaspoon ground ginger
1 teaspoon mustard powder
1.25 litres white vinegar
550g brown sugar

1 Combine apples, onions, dates, pepper, ginger, mustard and vinegar in large saucepan. Bring to boil, simmer, uncovered, for about 1 hour or until thick and pulpy. Add sugar; stir over heat, without boiling, until sugar is dissolved. Bring to boil, boil, uncovered, for 5 minutes.
2 Spoon hot chutney into hot sterilised jars; seal while hot.

makes about 1.25 litres

aubergine chutney

1 medium aubergine (300g),
   peeled, chopped coarsely
70g coarse cooking salt
2 cloves garlic, crushed
1 onion (150g), chopped
2 medium tomatoes (300g),
   deseeded, chopped coarsely

1 small green pepper (150g),
   chopped coarsely
125ml cider vinegar
125ml white vinegar
1 teaspoon chilli powder
1 teaspoon ground turmeric
110g brown sugar

1 Place aubergine in colander, sprinkle with salt; stand 30 minutes. Rinse aubergine, pat dry.
2 Combine aubergine, onion, tomato, pepper, garlic, vinegars, chilli and turmeric in large saucepan; simmer, uncovered, stirring occasionally, about 45 minutes or until vegetables are pulpy. Stir in sugar; cook, stirring, over low heat, until sugar dissolves.
3 Spoon hot chutney into hot sterilised jars; seal while hot.

makes about 750ml

date & tamarind chutney

75g dried tamarind
500ml boiling water
2 teaspoons vegetable oil
2 teaspoons black mustard seeds

2 teaspoons cumin seeds
500g fresh dates, stones removed,
   chopped
60ml malt vinegar

1 Combine tamarind and the boiling water in medium bowl; stand for 30 minutes. Strain tamarind over bowl, pressing to extract all liquid; discard tamarind. Heat oil in small pan; cook seeds, stirring, until they pop. Combine dates with tamarind liquid, seeds and vinegar in medium pan. Simmer, uncovered, 5 minutes until mixture is almost dry. Blend or process until almost smooth.
2 Spoon chutney into hot sterilised jars, seal while hot.

makes about 625ml

beetroot chutney

1kg beetroot, peeled, chopped
240g onions, chopped
800g apples, peeled, chopped
440g oranges, peeled,
    chopped
220g sugar

1 teaspoon grated lemon rind
2 tablespoons lemon juice
500ml white vinegar
1 small fresh red chilli, chopped
1 clove garlic, crushed
1 teaspoon coriander seeds

1 Steam or microwave beetroot until just tender.
2 Combine beetroot with remaining ingredients in large saucepan. Stir over heat, without boiling, until sugar is dissolved.
3 Bring to boil simmer, uncovered, stirring occasionally, for 1 hour, or until mixture is thick.
4 Spoon hot chutney into hot sterilised jars; seal while hot.

makes about 2 litres

spicy tomato chutney

1kg ripe tomatoes, peeled,
    chopped
400g apples, peeled,
    chopped
240g onions, chopped
375ml malt vinegar
220g brown sugar

¼ teaspoon chilli powder
½ teaspoon mustard powder
120g sultanas
1 clove garlic crushed
2 teaspoons curry powder
2 teaspoon ground allspice

1 Combine all ingredients in large saucepan.
2 Stir over heat, without boiling, until sugar is dissolved.
3 Bring to boil; simmer, uncovered, stirring occasionally, for I hour or until mixture is thick.
4 Spoon hot chutney into hot sterilised jars; seal while hot.

makes about 1.5 litres

chutneys & jams

ripe tomato & passionfruit jam

10 medium tomatoes (1kg), peeled, chopped
2 large apples (400g), peeled, chopped
80ml lemon juice
500ml passionfruit pulp (approximately 24)
1kg sugar

1   Combine tomatoes and apples in large saucepan, cook over low heat, stirring often, for about 25 minutes or until fruit is pulpy. Stir in juice, passionfruit pulp and sugar, stir over heat, without boiling, until sugar is dissolved. Bring to boil, boil, uncovered, without stirring, for about 30 minutes or until jam jells when tested.
2   Pour jam into hot sterilised jars; seal while hot.

makes about 1.25ml

green tomato chutney

1kg green tomatoes, chopped
240g onions, chopped
400g apples, chopped
1litre brown vinegar
550g brown sugar
240g sultanas
1½ teaspoons mustard powder
1 teaspoon ground cinnamon
¼ teaspoon ground cloves
¼ teaspoon cayenne pepper

1   Combine all ingredients in large saucepan. Stir over heat, without boiling, until sugar is dissolved. Bring to boil, simmer, uncovered, stirring occasionally, for 1½ hours or until mixture is thick.
2   Pour jam into hot sterilised jars; seal while hot.

makes about 1.5ml

chutneys & jams

spicy green tomato & apple jam

3 large apples (600g), peeled
5 medium green tomatoes (500g), peeled, chopped
250ml water
½ teaspoon ground ginger
½ teaspoon ground nutmeg
1 cinnamon stick
550g sugar, approximately

1 Chop apples, combine with tomatoes, water, ginger, nutmeg and cinnamon in a large saucepan. Bring to boil, simmer, covered, for about 30 minutes or until fruits are soft. Discard cinnamon stick.
2 Measure fruit mixture, allow 1 cup sugar to each cup of fruit mixture. Return fruit mixture and sugar to pan, stir over heat, without boiling, until sugar is dissolved. Bring to boil; boil, uncovered, without stirring, for about 15 minutes or until jam jells when tested.
3 Pour hot jam into hot sterilised jars; seal while hot.

makes about 750ml

chilli jam

750g fresh long red chillies, chopped coarsely
vegetable oil, for deep-frying
3 large onions (600g), chopped coarsely
16 shallots (400g), chopped coarsely
10 cloves garlic, peeled, chopped coarsely
10cm piece ginger (50g), peeled, chopped coarsely
200g coarsely chopped palm sugar
85g tamarind paste
80ml fish sauce

1 Deep-fry chillies, in batches, in hot oil until soft. Drain on
absorbent paper. Reheat oil; deep-fry combined onions, shallots,
garlic and ginger, in batches, until browned lightly. Drain on
absorbent paper.
2 Combine vegetables with 250ml of the cooking oil in large
bowl. Process, in batches, until almost smooth.
3 Cook chilli mixture in large heavy-based pan over low heat,
stirring, for about 10 minutes. Add sugar; cook, stirring, 10 minutes.
Add remaining ingredients; cook over low heat, stirring
occasionally, about 2 hours or until thick and dark red in colour.
4 Pour into hot sterilised jars; seal immediately.

makes about 1.5 litres
tips Chilli jam is really hot and a little goes a long way. If you want
to decrease the heat, remove the seeds from the chillies using
disposable gloves. The jam is best poured into small jars and
stored in a cool dark place. Once opened, store in the fridge.

lemon & mustard seed chutney

4 medium lemons (720g)
2 teaspoons coarse cooking salt
2 tablespoons white mustard seeds
2 medium onions (240g), chopped
250ml cider vinegar
1 teaspoon mixed spice
85g chopped raisins
220g sugar

1 Chop unpeeled lemons; discard seeds.
2 Combine lemons and salt in large bowl, cover, stand overnight.
3 Place mustard seeds in large saucepan, stir over heat until seeds have popped. Add undrained lemon mixture, onions, vinegar, spice, raisins and sugar; stir over heat, without boiling, until sugar is dissolved.
5 Bring to boil, simmer, uncovered, stirring occasionally, for 45 minutes or until mixture is thick.
6 Pour chutney into hot sterilised jars; seal while hot.

makes about 750ml

red onion jam

4 large red onions (1.2kg), sliced
375ml water
125ml malt vinegar
130g brown sugar
2 teaspoons finely grated orange rind
125ml orange juice

1   Combine onion and the water in large saucepan, bring to a
boil; boil, uncovered, stirring occasionally, about 20 minutes or until
onion is soft and liquid has evaporated.
2   Add remaining ingredients; stir over heat, without boiling, until
sugar is dissolved.
3   Simmer, covered, 30 minutes. Remove cover; simmer, stirring
occasionally, further 30 minutes or until mixture thickens.
4   Spoon jam into hot sterilised jars; seal while hot.

makes about 500ml

Microwave
chutneys

dried fruit chutney

200g dried pears, chopped
200g dried apricots, chopped
200g pitted dates, chopped
180g dried apples, chopped
240g sultanas
500ml water
400g brown sugar

500ml cider vinegar
½ teaspoon chilli powder
½ teaspoon ground turmeric
½ teaspoon ground nutmeg
½ teaspoon ground ginger
1 clove garlic, crushed

1   Combine dried fruits with the water in large glass microwave-safe bowl; cook, covered, on HIGH (100%) for 10 minutes, stirring once during cooking. Stand, covered, 10 minutes. Add sugar, stir until sugar dissolves.
2   Add remaining ingredients; cook, uncovered, on HIGH (100%) for about 30 minutes or until mixture is thick, stirring 3 times during cooking.
3   Spoon chutney into hot sterilised jars; seal while hot.

makes about 1.75 litres

tomato jam

4 medium tomatoes (750g),
   peeled
1 small apple (130g), peeled,
   grated coarsely

75g finely chopped stem
   ginger
60ml lemon juice
440g caster sugar

1   Roughly chop tomatoes, combine with apple and ginger in large glass microwave-safe bowl; cook, uncovered, on HIGH (100%) for about 15 minutes or until mixture is pulpy.
2   Add juice and sugar, stir until sugar dissolves. Cook, uncovered, on HIGH (100%) for about 20 minutes or until jam jells when tested, stirring 3 times during cooking.
3   Pour jam into hot sterilised jars; seal while hot.

makes about 625ml

Relishes

oriental relish

1 medium lemon (180g)
1 large orange (220g)
1 medium onion (120g), grated
2 x 425g cans tomatoes
600g apples, peeled, chopped
1 cinnamon stick

2 star anise
2 tablespoons grated fresh ginger
1 teaspoon ground allspice
½ teaspoon cardamom seeds
330g brown sugar
180ml malt vinegar
250ml water

1 Chop unpeeled lemon and orange; discard seeds. Blend or process lemon and orange until almost smooth.
2 Combine lemon mixture, onion, undrained crushed tomatoes and remaining ingredients in large saucepan. Stir over heat, without boiling, until sugar is dissolved. Bring to boil, simmer, uncovered, stirring occasionally, for 1½ hours or until mixture is thick. Discard cinnamon sticks and star anise.
3 Spoon hot relish into hot sterilised jars; seal while hot.

makes about 1.75 litres

corn relish

3 x 440g cans corn kernels,
  drained
3 small onions (240g), chopped
1 small red pepper (150g),
  chopped
1 small green pepper (150g),
  chopped
2 sticks celery (150g), chopped
500ml cider vinegar

430ml white vinegar
220g sugar
1 tablespoon mustard powder
1 tablespoon yellow mustard
  seeds
1 teaspoon ground turmeric
½ teaspoon ground cloves
35g cornflour
60ml white vinegar, extra

1   Combine corn, onion, peppers, celery, vinegars, sugar, mustard,
seeds, turmeric and cloves in large saucepan. Bring to a boil;
simmer, uncovered, about 45 minutes, stirring occasionally, or until
mixture thickens slightly. Stir in blended cornflour and extra vinegar,
stir until mixture boils and thickens.
2   Pour relish into hot sterilised jars; seal while hot.

makes about 1.5 litres

cranberry & red onion relish

50g butter
3 large red onions (900g),
   sliced thinly
1kg frozen cranberries
440g brown sugar

250ml malt vinegar
125ml balsamic vinegar
1 teaspoon coarse cooking salt
4 whole cloves
½ teaspoon dried chilli flakes

1 Melt butter in large saucepan; cook onion, stirring, until soft.
2 Add remaining ingredients; stir over heat until sugar dissolves.
Bring to the boil; reduce heat. Simmer, uncovered, stirring
occasionally, for about 1 hour or until thick.
3 Pour hot relish into hot sterilised jars; seal while hot.

makes 1.5 litres

blackberry relish

1kg blackberries
125ml water
1 tablespoon sugar
1 teaspoon mustard powder

1 teaspoon ground allspice
½ teaspoon ground cinnamon
250ml malt vinegar

1 Combine half the blackberries and the water in large pan.
Bring to boil, simmer, covered, for 10 minutes or until berries are
soft. Blend or process mixture until smooth, return to pan.
2 Stir in remaining ingredients. Bring to boil, simmer, uncovered,
stirring occasionally, for 15 minutes or until mixture is thick.
3 Pour relish into hot sterilised jars;
seal while hot

makes about 1 litre

relishes

papaya & chilli relish

½ teaspoon black peppercorns
½ teaspoon pimentos
1½kg papaya, chopped
400g apples, peeled, chopped
400g tomatoes, peeled,
    chopped

440g sugar
750ml white vinegar
2 teaspoons coarse cooking salt
3 small fresh red chillies,
    chopped
2 teaspoons grated fresh ginger

1 Tie peppercorns and pimentos in piece of muslin, combine muslin bag with remaining ingredients in large saucepan. Stir over heat, without boiling, until sugar is dissolved. Bring to boil, simmer, uncovered for 1½ hours or until mixture is thick. Discard muslin bag.
2 Pour relish into hot sterilised jars; seal while hot.

makes about 1.25 litres

sugar-free courgette relish

3 medium courgettes (500g),
    chopped
1 medium onion (120g),
    chopped
1 medium red pepper (150g),
    chopped

500ml water
125ml white vinegar
1 tablespoon mustard powder
1 tablespoon artificial sweetener
1½ tablespoons cornflour
2 tablespoons water, extra

1 Combine courgette, onion, pepper, water, vinegar, mustard and sweetener in large saucepan. Bring to boil, simmer, covered, for 10 minutes or until courgette is soft.
2 Stir in blended cornflour and extra water, stir over heat until mixture boils and thickens.
3 Pour relish into hot sterilised jars; seal while hot.

makes about 1.25 litres
tip This relish will keep in the fridge for 4 weeks.

roasted pepper relish

3 medium red peppers (450g)
3 medium green peppers (450g)
500ml water
125ml white vinegar
110g brown sugar
1 medium onion (120g), chopped
1 small fresh red chilli, chopped
1 tablespoon cornflour
2 tablespoons water, extra

1 Cut peppers in half lengthways, remove seeds. Place peppers, cut side down, on oven tray. Cook under hot grill until skins blister and blacken; cover with paper or cling film and leave to cool. Remove and discard skins, chop pepper flesh.
2 Combine vinegar, sugar and the water in large saucepan. Stir over heat without boiling, until sugar is dissolved. Stir in peppers, onion, and chilli.
3 Bring to boil, simmer, covered, for 10 minutes. Stir in blended cornflour and extra water, stir until mixture boils and thickens.
4 Pour relish into hot sterilised jars; seal while hot.

makes about 500ml

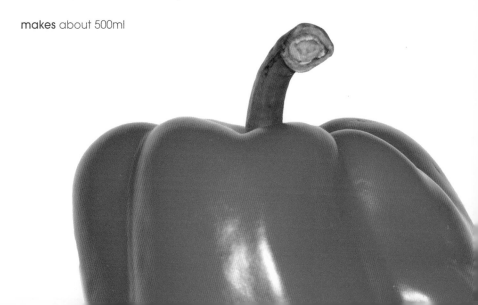

Microwave
relishes

spicy onion & tomato relish

6 medium (1.1kg) tomatoes,
  chopped
2 medium (300g) onions, chopped
  finely
2 medium (300g) apples, peeled,
  chopped finely
1 teaspoon salt
1 teaspoon finely grated lemon rind

1 teaspoon mustard powder
1 teaspoon garam masala
2 tablespoons mild curry powder
250g brown sugar
125ml white vinegar
60ml lemon juice
1 tablespoon tomato paste

1 Combine all ingredients in large glass microwave-safe bowl; cook, uncovered, on HIGH (100%) about 1 hour or until mixture thickens, stirring three times during cooking.
2 Spoon hot relish into hot sterilised jars; seal while hot.

makes about 1 litre

green tomato relish

6 large (1.5kg) green tomatoes,
  chopped
2 medium (300g) onions, chopped
2 cloves garlic, crushed
250ml cider vinegar
60ml malt vinegar
220g sugar

2 teaspoons salt
1 teaspoon ground ginger
4 cloves
½ teaspoon ground cardamom
½ teaspoon ground cinnamon
½ teaspoon ground turmeric

1 Combine all ingredients in large glass microwave-safe bowl; cook, uncovered, on HIGH (100%) about 5 minutes or until sugar dissolves, stirring three times during cooking.
2 Cook relish, uncovered, on HIGH (100%) about 1¼ hours or until mixture thickens, stirring three times during cooking.
3 Spoon hot relish into hot sterilised jars; seal while hot.

makes about 1 litre

Pickles

Note We haven't specified the quantities the pickles will make in some of these recipes as it depends on the chopped size of the vegetables and how tightly they are packed in the jars.

piccalilli

½ small cauliflower (350g), chopped coarsely
2 medium carrots (240g), sliced thinly
2 trimmed celery sticks (150g), sliced thickly
2 small green tomatoes (260g), chopped coarsely
1 large cucumber (400g), sliced thickly
10 baby onions (250g), quartered
260g coarse cooking salt
1.25 litres white vinegar
220g sugar
1 tablespoon ground turmeric
1 tablespoon mustard powder
½ teaspoon ground ginger
2 cloves garlic, crushed
2 red thai chillies, deseeded, chopped finely
35g cornflour
60ml white vinegar, extra

1 Combine cauliflower, carrot, celery, tomato, cucumber, onion and salt in large bowl. Cover; stand overnight.
2 Rinse vegetables under cold water; drain well. Combine vinegar, sugar, turmeric, mustard powder, ginger, garlic and chilli in large saucepan; bring to a boil. Add vegetables; simmer, covered, about 5 minutes or until vegetables are just tender. Stir in blended cornflour and extra vinegar; stir over heat until mixture boils and thickens.
3 Spoon hot piccalilli into hot sterilised jars; seal while hot.

makes about 3 litres

gherkins in spiced vinegar

1.5 litres water
180g coarse cooking salt
2kg gherkin cucumbers
spiced vinegar
1 litre white vinegar
495g sugar
2 cinnamon sticks
2 teaspoons black peppercorns
2 teaspoons cloves

1 Combine water and salt in large saucepan, stir over heat until salt is dissolved; cool.

2 Wash gherkins well, place in large bowl, cover gherkins completely with salt water, cover, stand 48 hours.

3 Drain gherkins, rinse under cold water. Pack gherkins in large sterilised jar, cover completely with spiced vinegar; seal.

spiced vinegar Combine all ingredients in saucepan, stir over heat, without boiling, until sugar is dissolved. Bring to boil, simmer mixture 2 minutes, stand 5 minutes, strain, cool.

pickled apples

660g sugar
625ml white vinegar
1 teaspoon ground cinnamon
1kg apples, peeled, quartered

1 Combine sugar, vinegar and cinnamon in large saucepan. Stir over heat, without boiling, until sugar is dissolved.
2 Add apples, bring to boil; simmer, uncovered, stirring occasionally, for 10 minutes or until apples are just tender.
3 Pack apples into large hot sterilised jars, pour over vinegar mixture to cover apples completely; seal while hot. The apples will absorb some of the liquid on standing.

tomato & apple pickle

1kg tomatoes, peeled, chopped
1 large apple (200g), chopped
1 onion (120g), chopped
1 tablespoon ground ginger
3 black peppercorns
3 teaspoons white mustard seeds
375ml white vinegar
220g brown sugar

1 Combine all ingredients in large saucepan, stir over heat, without boiling, until sugar is dissolved.
2 Bring to boil; simmer, uncovered, stirring occasionally, for 45 minutes or until mixture is thick.
3 Pour mixture into hot sterilised jars; seal while hot.

tomato kasaundi

4 large tomatoes (880g),
   chopped coarsely
1 medium onion (150g), chopped
   coarsely
75g brown sugar
4 cloves garlic, chopped coarsely
3cm piece fresh ginger (15g),
   chopped finely

4 fresh small red thai chillies,
   chopped coarsely
2 teaspoons ground cumin
½ teaspoon ground turmeric
½ teaspoon chilli powder
¼ teaspoon ground cloves
2 tablespoons vegetable oil
60ml white vinegar

1 Blend or process ingredients until smooth. Transfer mixture to
large pan; cook, stirring, without boiling, until sugar is dissolved.
Simmer, uncovered, stirring occasionally, about 45 minutes or until
kasaundi thickens slightly.
2 Pour hot kasaundi into hot sterilised jars; seal while hot.

makes about 750ml

spicy mustard pickles

¼ medium cauliflower (400g), chopped coarsely
250g green beans, trimmed, chopped coarsely
3 medium onions (450g), sliced thickly
1 medium red pepper (200g), sliced thickly
70g coarse cooking salt
2 teaspoons mustard powder
2 tablespoons wholegrain mustard
3 teaspoons curry powder
¼ teaspoon ground turmeric
500ml white vinegar
220g brown sugar
2 tablespoons plain flour

1 Combine vegetables and salt in large bowl. Cover; stand overnight.
2 Rinse vegetables; drain. Stir vegetables, mustards, curry powder, turmeric, 430ml of the vinegar and sugar in large saucepan over heat, without boiling, until sugar dissolves; bring to a boil. Simmer, uncovered, about 10 minutes or until vegetables are just tender.
3 Stir in blended flour and remaining vinegar; stir over heat until mixture boils and thickens. Pour into hot sterilised jars; seal. while hot

makes 1 litre

red bean & pepper pickles

375g dried red kidney beans
300g red peppers, chopped
300g green peppers, chopped
500g cauliflower, chopped
400g green beans, copped
1litre malt vinegar
330g brown sugar

2 tablespoons mustard powder
3 tablespoons white mustard
  seeds
2 teaspoons turmeric
310g corn kernels
35g plain flour
80ml water

1 Combine kidney beans with water in large bowl, stand overnight.
2 Rinse vegetables under cold water; drain. Add beans to large saucepan of boiling water, boil, uncovered, for 1 hour or until tender, drain. Boil, steam or microwave peppers, cauliflower and green beans until just soft.
3 Combine vinegar, sugar, mustard powder, mustard seeds and turmeric in large saucepan. Stir over heat, without boiling, until sugar is dissolved. Add kidney beans, corn and vegetables with blended flour and water, stir over heat until mixture boils and thickens.
4 Pour mixture into hot sterilised jars; seal while hot.

makes 1.75 litres

spicy pickled onions

2kg pickling onions
780g coarse cooking salt
1.25 litres white vinegar
1 tablespoon coarse cooking salt, extra
1 tablespoon sugar
1½ teaspoons cloves
2 teaspoons allspice
2 teaspoons black peppercorns

1 Place unpeeled onions and salt in large bowl, add enough water to just float the onions. Cover; stand 2 days, stirring occasionally. Drain onions, discard liquid. Peel onions carefully, leaving ends intact.
2 Place onions in large heatproof bowl. Cover with boiling water, stand 3 minutes; drain. Repeat this process twice. Pack hot onions firmly into hot sterilised jars.
3 Bring remaining ingredients to a boil in medium saucepan; simmer, uncovered, 15 minutes. Pour hot vinegar mixture over onions in jars to cover completely; seal while hot.

aubergine pickle

2 large aubergines (1kg)
2 teaspoons salt
2 teaspoons ground turmeric
500ml vegetable oil
1 tablespoon black mustard
  seeds
125ml malt vinegar
5 cloves garlic, crushed
2 tablespoons grated fresh
  ginger

1 large onion (200g), chopped
1 teaspoon ground fennel
2 teaspoons ground cumin
1 tablespoon ground coriander
4 tablespoons tamarind
  concentrate
2 teaspoons dried chilli flakes
1 cinnamon stick
2 teaspoons palm sugar

1 Wash aubergines; cut into 2cm cubes. Place aubergine in colander in sink, stir in combined salt and turmeric; stand 1 hour. Pat aubergine cubes dry with absorbent paper.

2 Heat oil in large frying pan; cook aubergine, in batches, until soft. Drain cooked aubergine on absorbent paper. Reserve oil used for cooking.

3 Blend or process seeds and vinegar, then add garlic, ginger and onion; blend until smooth.

4 In heated small frying pan, dry-fry ground spices until fragrant. Heat 180ml reserved oil in large saucepan, add aubergine, vinegar mixture, spice mixture, tamarind, chilli and cinnamon; simmer, covered, 20 minutes. Stir in sugar. Remove cinnamon stick.

5 Place mixture into jar; seal while hot.

makes 1.25 litres
tip The tamarind tree produces clusters of hairy brown pods, each of which is filled with seeds and a viscous pulp, that are dried and pressed into the blocks of tamarind concentrate. It gives a sweet-sour, slightly astringent taste to the pickle.

italian pickled vegetables

2 medium red peppers (400g)
1 litre white vinegar
500ml water
6 black peppercorns
1 bay leaf
1 tablespoon sea salt flakes
1 small aubergine (230g), quartered lengthways, cut into 1cm slices
½ small cauliflower (200g), cut into florets
2 medium carrots (240g), sliced thinly diagonally
2 stalks celery (300g), trimmed, sliced thickly diagonally
2 tablespoons finely chopped fresh flat-leaf parsley
2 teaspoons finely chopped fresh thyme
500ml olive oil
2 cloves garlic, sliced thinly

1 Preheat oven to 200°C/180°C fan-assisted. Quarter peppers; discard seeds and membranes. Roast pepper, skin-side up, until skin blisters and blackens. Cover with cling film or paper for 5 minutes; peel away skin then slice flesh thickly.
2 Meanwhile, combine vinegar, the water, peppercorns, bay leaf and half the salt in large saucepan; heat without boiling. Add aubergine, cauliflower, carrot and celery; bring to the boil. Reduce heat; simmer, uncovered, about 5 minutes or until vegetables are tender. Drain vegetables; discard liquid.
3 Combine hot vegetables, pepper, herbs and remaining salt in large heatproof bowl. Spoon vegetable mixture into hot sterilised jars.
4 Heat oil and garlic in small pan, strain into large heatproof jug; discard garlic. Carefully pour hot oil into jar to completely cover vegetables, leaving a 1cm space at top of jar. Seal while hot.

makes about 1.5 litres
tip Store in the refrigerator for up to three months. Serve with crusty bread or as part of an antipasto platter with cheeses and deli meats.

pickled beetroot

6 medium beetroot (1kg)
220g sugar
1 litre cider vinegar
1 small cinnamon stick
8 black peppercorns
4 small dried chillies
1 teaspoon black mustard seeds

1 Trim beetroot, leaving 3cm of the stem attached. Wash carefully. Add beetroot to large pan of cold water; boil 45 minutes or until tender. Cool in cooking water; reserve 125ml of the liquid.
2 Rub skin off beetroot; quarter, then place in hot sterilised jars.
3 Combine reserved cooking liquid, sugar, vinegar and remaining ingredients in large pan; stir over heat, without boiling, until sugar is dissolved; bring to a boil. Pour liquid over beetroot; seal while hot.

makes about 2 litres (24 pieces)

spicy orange segments

2kg oranges, segmented
250ml cider vinegar
125ml water
2 cinnamon sticks
½ teaspoon cloves
125ml orange juice
440g sugar

1 Layer orange segments into hot sterilised jar.
2 Combine remaining ingredients in saucepan, stir over heat, without boiling, until sugar is dissolved.
3 Bring to boil, simmer 1 minute, pour over orange slices to cover completely. Seal while hot.

marinated mushrooms

1 litre white vinegar
250ml dry white wine
1 tablespoon sea salt flakes
800g button mushrooms, halved
2 cloves garlic, sliced thinly
½ teaspoon dried chilli flakes
1 tablespoon coarsely chopped fresh rosemary
1 tablespoon finely chopped flat-leaf parsley
3 x 5cm strips lemon rind
1 bay leaf
500ml olive oil

1 Combine vinegar, wine and half the salt in medium saucepan; heat without boiling. Add mushrooms; simmer, uncovered, about 5 minutes or until tender. Drain mushrooms; discard liquid.

2 Combine hot mushrooms, garlic, chilli, herbs, rind, bay leaf and remaining salt in large heatproof bowl. Spoon mixture into hot sterilised jars.

3 Heat oil in small pan; carefully pour into jar to completely cover mushrooms, leaving a 1cm space at top of jar. Seal while hot.

makes about 1 litre
tip Store in refrigerator for up to three months.

pickled quail eggs & beetroot

12 quail eggs
500g baby beetroot, leaves trimmed
1 litre cider vinegar
165g caster sugar
2 bay leaves
1 tablespoon black peppercorns
2 teaspoons finely grated fresh horseradish
3 tablespoons fresh dill leaves

1 Add eggs to small saucepan of boiling water; simmer, uncovered, about 6 minutes. Drain, then shell eggs.
2 Trim leaves from beetroot; place unpeeled beetroot in large saucepan of boiling water. Boil, covered, about 20 minutes or until beetroot are tender. Cool beetroot 10 minutes then peel.
3 Combine vinegar, sugar, bay leaves, peppercorns and horseradish in medium saucepan; stir over heat until sugar dissolves then bring to the boil. Remove from heat, stir in dill.
4 Place eggs and beetroot in hot sterilised jar; pour in enough vinegar mixture to cover eggs and beetroot. Seal jar; cool.

serves 6
tip This pickle will keep in the refrigerator for up to 1 week.

pickled bananas

180ml white vinegar
330g brown sugar
1½ teaspoons grated lemon rind
8 cloves
3 cardamom pods, bruised
½ teaspoon cracked mixed peppercorns
pinch saffron powder
½ teaspoon ground nutmeg
2kg firm bananas

1 Combine vinegar, sugar, rind, cloves, cardamom, peppercorns, saffron and nutmeg in large saucepan. Stir over heat, without boiling, until sugar is dissolved.
2 Bring to boil; boil, uncovered, for 5 minutes. Simmer, covered, for further 5 minutes.
3 Peel and slice bananas, pack into hot sterilised jars. Strain hot liquid into jar to cover bananas completely. Seal while hot.

pickled olives

1.5kg fresh black or green olives
75g fine sea salt
1 litre water
125ml olive oil

1 Discard any over-blemished olives. Using a sharp knife, make two cuts lengthways in each olive, through to stone.
2 Place olives in 2-litre sterilised jars until jars are two-thirds full; cover olives with cold water. To keep olives submerged, fill a small plastic bag with cold water, tie bag securely, sit on top of olives in jar. Scum will appear on surface of water. Change water in jars daily, refilling with fresh, cold water. Change water for 4 days with black olives, 6 days with green olives.
3 Combine sea salt and the 1 litre of water in medium saucepan, stir over heat until salt is dissolved; cool. Discard water in jars; fill with enough salted water to cover olives. Pour enough oil in jars to cover completely; seal jars.

makes about 2 litres
tip These will be ready to eat after about 5 weeks sealed in salted water; do not mix green and black varieties of olives when pickling them.

marinated olives

600g black or green pickled olives, drained
1 clove garlic, sliced
2 lemon wedges
1 sprig fresh dill
500ml olive oil

1   Combine olives, garlic, lemon and dill in 1-litre hot sterilised jar, add enough oil to cover olives; seal jar.

makes about 1 litre
tip Olives must be pickled before they can be marinated; after being marinated 2 weeks, olives will be ready to eat.

chilli plum sauce

14 medium plums (1kg), chopped
275g sugar
500ml white vinegar
2 small fresh red chillies, chopped
1 teaspoon coarse cooking salt
1 teaspoon ground ginger
½ teaspoon cayenne pepper
8 cloves

1 Combine plums and stones with remaining ingredients in large saucepan, stir over heat, without boiling, until sugar is dissolved. Bring to boil, simmer, uncovered, stirring occasionally, for about 40 minutes or until mixture is pulpy; strain.
2 Return mixture to pan, bring to boil, simmer, uncovered, for about 10 minutes or until mixture is slightly thickened.
3 Pour sauce into hot sterilised jars; seal while hot.

makes about 750ml

plum sauce

20 medium (1.5kg) plums, pitted, chopped
330g brown sugar
500ml malt vinegar
1 teaspoon cloves
2 cinnamon sticks
2 star anise
5cm piece fresh ginger, peeled, bruised

1   Combine plums, sugar and vinegar in large saucepan, stir over heat, without boiling, until sugar is dissolved. Tie cloves, cinnamon, star anise and ginger in piece of muslin; add to pan. Bring to boil, simmer, uncovered, stirring occasionally, for about 45 minutes or until thick. Discard muslin bag.
2   Pour sauce into hot sterilised jars; seal while hot.

makes about 750ml

home-made worcestershire sauce

750ml malt vinegar
180g treacle
160g plum jam
1 small onion (75g), chopped
1 clove garlic, crushed
¼ teaspoon chilli powder
1 teaspoon ground allspice
¼ teaspoon ground cloves
¼ teaspoon cayenne pepper

1   Combine all ingredients in large saucepan. Stir over heat until mixture boils, simmer, uncovered, for 1 hour, stirring occasionally.
2   Strain mixture into hot sterilised jars; seal while hot.

makes about 500ml

barbecue sauce

2 tablespoons oil
2 cloves garlic, crushed
2 medium onions (240g),
    chopped
1 small fresh red chilli, chopped
4 medium ripe tomatoes
    (400g), chopped
1 large apple (200g), chopped

1 celery stick, chopped
125ml dry red wine
2 tablespoons brown sugar
1 tablespoon seeded mustard
¼ teaspoon coarse cooking salt
¼ teaspoon ground black
    pepper
1 tablespoon malt vinegar

1 Heat oil in saucepan, add garlic, onions and chilli, cook until onions are soft. Stir in remaining ingredients, bring to boil, simmer, uncovered, stirring occasionally, for about 30 minutes or until mixture is thick.
2 Blend or process mixture until smooth, push through fine sieve; discard pulp. Pour sauce into hot sterilised jars; seal while hot.

makes about 500ml

mild tomato sauce

3kg ripe tomatoes, chopped
3 onions (360g), chopped
2 large apples (400g),
    chopped

250ml white vinegar
250ml water
1 nutmeg
440g sugar

1 Combine tomatoes, onions, apples, vinegar, water and nutmeg in large saucepan. Bring to boil, simmer, uncovered, stirring occasionally, for about 1 hour or until thick. Add sugar, stir over heat, without boiling, until sugar is dissolved.
2 Blend or process mixture in several batches until smooth; push through fine sieve. Discard pulp.
3 Pour into hot sterilised jars; seal while hot.

makes about 1.5 litres

sweet chilli tomato sauce

4 large tomatoes (1kg), peeled, chopped
1 teaspoon salt
4 cloves garlic, chopped
60ml balsamic vinegar
55g sugar
3 tablespoons chopped fresh coriander leaves
3 small fresh red chillies, chopped

1 Combine all ingredients in large glass microwave-safe bowl. Cook, uncovered, on HIGH (100%) about 25 minutes or until sauce thickens, stirring twice during cooking; cool 5 minutes.
2 Blend or process sauce until smooth. Pour into hot sterilised bottles; seal while hot.

makes about 625ml

green tomato sauce

10 medium green tomatoes (1kg), chopped
4 shallots, chopped
125ml water
1 tablespoon caraway seeds
2 teaspoons turmeric
2 teaspoons mixed spice
½ teaspoon ground ginger
250ml water, extra
330g sugar
250ml malt vinegar

1 Combine tomatoes, shallots and water in large saucepan, bring to boil, simmer, covered, for about 20 minutes or until tomatoes are pulpy.
2 Blend or process mixture in several batches until smooth, return to pan. Stir in remaining ingredients, stir over heat, without boiling, until sugar is dissolved. Bring to boil, simmer, uncovered, stirring occasionally, for about 45 minutes or until mixture is thick.
3 Pour sauce into hot sterilised jars; seal while hot.

makes about 1.25 litres

raspberry cider sauce

2kg raspberries
625ml cider vinegar
1 teaspoon dijon mustard
½ teaspoon mixed spice
670g sugar

1 Combine raspberries and vinegar in large saucepan. Bring to boil, simmer, uncovered, for 15 minutes. Stir in mustard and spice, simmer further 30 minutes. Strain mixture into clean pan through fine sieve; discard seeds.
2 Stir in sugar, stir over heat, without boiling, until sugar is dissolved. Bring to boil, simmer, uncovered, stirring occasionally, for 30 minutes.
3 Pour sauce into hot sterilised jars; seal while hot.

makes about 1 litre

mustard sauce

125ml vegetable oil
3 tablespoons white mustard
   seeds, crushed
4 eggs
1½ tablespoons mustard
   powder

55g sugar
1 teaspoon coarse cooking salt
½ teaspoon cracked black
   peppercorns
2 teaspoons plain flour
250ml white vinegar

1 Heat oil in pan, add seeds, cook until lightly browned; cool.
2 Blend or process eggs, dry mustard, sugar, salt, peppercorns and flour until smooth. With motor operating, pour in vinegar in a thin stream, then pour in mustard seed mixture in a thin stream.
3 Transfer mixture to pan, stir over heat until mixture boils and thickens slightly. Pour sauce into hot sterilised jars; seal while hot

makes about 500ml

rich fruit sauce

1.75kg tomatoes, chopped
5 large apples (1 kg), chopped
4 onions (480g), chopped
250g dates, chopped
750g raisins
1 litre white vinegar
1 teaspoon mixed spice
2 teaspoons white mustard seeds
¼ teaspoon cayenne pepper
2 small fresh red chillies, chopped
440g brown sugar

1 Combine all ingredients except sugar in large saucepan. Bring to boil, simmer, covered, for about 1 hour or until mixture is pulpy.
2 Push mixture through coarse sieve, return mixture to pan, stir in sugar. Stir over heat, without boiling, until sugar is dissolved. Bring to boil, simmer, uncovered, stirring occasionally, for about 1 hour or until sauce thickens slightly.
3 Pour into hot sterilised jars; seal while hot.

makes about 2 litres

tapenade

1 tablespoon drained capers, rinsed
3 anchovy fillets, drained
60g pitted black olives
60ml olive oil

1 Blend or process ingredients until desired consistency is reached.

makes 125ml

tomato & olive tapenade

150g drained sun-dried tomatoes
80ml olive oil
2 tablespoons red wine vinegar
1 tablespoon brown sugar
1 tablespoon coarsely chopped
oregano
1 tablespoon coarsely chopped
basil
½ teaspoon cracked black pepper
80g roasted pecans
40g pitted black olives

1 Blend or process ingredients until smooth.

makes 330ml

pesto

2 cups firmly packed fresh
basil leaves
80g roasted pine nuts
2 cloves garlic, quartered
125ml olive oil
25g finely grated parmesan

1 Process basil, nuts and
garlic until chopped finely.
With motor operating, add
oil in thin, steady stream until
combined. Add cheese;
process until combined.

makes 310ml

coriander pesto

2 tablespoons unsalted roasted
peanuts
2 cloves garlic, quartered
½ cup firmly packed fresh
coriander leaves
125ml groundnut oil

1 Blend or process nuts, garlic
and coriander until chopped
finely. With motor operating,
add oil in thin, steady stream
until combined.

makes 165ml

irish crème liqueur

1 tablespoon instant coffee granules
1 tablespoon boiling water
1½ tablespoons chocolate-flavoured topping
350ml Irish whiskey
460ml double cream
395g can condensed milk
1 egg
1 teaspoon coconut essence

1 Dissolve coffee in the water in a large jug; stir in topping.
2 Whisk in remaining ingredients. Strain mixture into cooled sterilised bottles; seal immediately.
3 Store liqueur in refrigerator for up to 6 months.

makes 1.25 litres

cherry brandy liqueur

500g cherries, pitted
220g sugar
750ml brandy
1 cinnamon stick

1 Combine cherries and sugar in large sterilised jar, cover with tight-fitting lid, stand 2 to 3 days; shake jar daily until juice begins to appear.
2 Add brandy and cinnamon to jar, seal tightly, stand 3 months in cool dark place, shaking jar occasionally.
3 Strain cherries through fine cloth, reserve liquid, discard pulp. Pour liquid into sterilised bottles; seal immediately.

makes about 1 litre

other preserves

These recipes are a treat at Christmas time. You can drink the flavoured vodka or brandy as you would a liqueur, or serve the cherries or cumquats with cream or ice-cream and a little of the liqueur.

brandied cumquats

750g cumquats
2 cinnamon sticks, halved lengthways
2 vanilla pods, halved lengthways
660g caster sugar
625ml brandy

1 Wash and dry the cumquats well, then prick each one several times with a fine skewer or a thick needle.
2 Place the cumquats, cinnamon and vanilla in clean, sterilised jars; pour over enough of the combined sugar and brandy to cover the cumquats completely. Seal.
3 Stand the jars in a cool, dark place for at least 2 months before using. Invert the jars every few days to help dissolve the sugar.

makes 1.75 litres

cherries in vodka

500g fresh cherries, pitted
165g caster sugar
500ml vodka, approximately

1 Layer cherries and sugar in sterilised jars; pour over enough vodka to cover cherries completely. Seal.
2 Stand in cool dark place for at least six weeks before using. Invert jars occasionally to help dissolve the sugar.

makes 1 litre
tips The cherries will last indefinitely. Do not allow metal lids to touch the liquid; use plastic or glass instead. This recipe is best made four to six weeks ahead of using.

preserved lemons

10 medium lemons (1.4kg), quartered
250g salt
1 bay leaf, torn
1 cinnamon stick, quartered
1 teaspoon coriander seeds, bruised
500ml lemon juice

1 Combine lemons and salt in large bowl.
2 Pack lemon mixture, bay leaf, cinnamon and seeds firmly into two (750ml) sterilised jars. Pour in enough juice to cover lemons completely; seal jars tightly.
3 Stand in cool, dry place at least a month.

tips You will need around 8 lemons to make 500ml juice. We used fine sea salt, but coarse cooking or table salt can also be used. Preserved lemon is a North African speciality. When recipes call for preserved lemon, use only the rind; scrape away and discard the lemon flesh.

mincemeat

1kg sultanas
375g currants
425g raisins, chopped
250g pitted dried dates, chopped
250g pitted prunes, chopped
250g glacé cherries, quartered
125g glacé apricots, chopped
115g glacé pineapple, chopped
115g stem ginger, chopped

120g mixed peel
3 apples (450g), peeled, grated
240g fig jam
2 tablespoons finely grated
   orange rind
60ml lemon juice
440g brown sugar
1 tablespoon mixed spice
330ml Grand Marnier

1 Combine ingredients in large bowl; cover tightly with cling film.
2 Store mixture in cool, dark place for a month (or longer) before using;
stir mixture every two or three days.

glossary

allspice also known as pimento; available whole or ground.

bay leaves aromatic leaves from the bay tree available fresh or dried; used to add a strong, slightly peppery flavour to dishes.

capers the grey-green buds of a warm climate shrub sold either dried and salted or pickled in vinegar brine.

caraway seeds a member of the parsley family; available in seed or ground form.

cardamom can be bought in pod, seed or ground form. Has a distinctive, aromatic, sweetly rich flavour.

cayenne pepper thin-fleshed, very hot red chilli; usually comes dried and ground.

chillies available in many types and sizes, both fresh and dried. The smaller the chilli, the hotter it is. Wear rubber gloves when handling chillies, as they can burn your skin. Removing seeds and membranes lessens the heat level.

chilli powder the Asian variety is the hottest, made from ground chillies; it can be used as a substitute for fresh chillies in the proportion ½ teaspoon ground chilli powder to 1 medium chopped fresh chilli.

cinnamon dried inner bark of the shoots of the cinnamon tree. Available as a stick or ground.

cloves can be used whole or in ground form. Has a strong scent and taste so should be used minimally.

condensed milk a canned milk product consisting of milk with more than half the water content removed and sugar added to the milk that remains.

coriander a fragrant herb; coriander seeds and ground coriander must never be used to replace fresh coriander or vice versa. The tastes are completely different.

cornflour also known as cornstarch; used as a thickening agent in cooking.

cumin available both ground and as whole seeds; cumin has a warm, earthy, rather strong flavour.

cumquat fruit resembling a small, oval orange.

curry powder a blend of ground spices; choose mild or hot to suit your taste and the recipe.

date fruit of the date palm, eaten fresh or dried. About 4cm to 6cm in length, oval and plump, thin-skinned, with a honey-sweet flavour and sticky texture.

dill also known as dill weed; used fresh or dried, in seed form or ground; has a sweet anise/celery flavour with distinctive feathery, frond-like fresh leaves.

fennel seeds dried seeds with a liquorice flavour.

figs small, soft, pear-shaped fruit with a sweet pulpy flesh full of tiny edible seeds.

fish sauce made from pulverised salted fermented fish, mostly anchovies. Has a pungent smell and strong taste; use sparingly.

flat-leaf parsley also known as continental parsley or italian parsley.

garam masala a blend of spices based on varying proportions of cardamom, cinnamon, cloves, coriander, fennel and cumin, roasted and ground together. Black pepper and chilli can be added for a hotter version.

ginger

fresh also called green or root ginger; the thick gnarled root of a tropical plant.

stem fresh ginger root preserved in sugar syrup.

glacé fruit fruit such as cherries, peaches, pineapple, orange and citron cooked in heavy sugar syrup then dried.

golden syrup a by-product of refined sugarcane; pure maple syrup or honey can be substituted.

grand marnier a brandy-based orange-flavoured liqueur.

horseradish pungent plant root that is grated and mixed with vinegar, and sometimes cream, to make a sauce.

mixed peel candied citrus peel.

mixed spice a blend of ground spices, usually cinnamon, allspice and nutmeg.

mustard

dijon a pale brown, distinctively flavoured fairly mild French mustard.

powder finely ground white (yellow) mustard seeds.

wholegrain a French-style coarse-grain mustard made from crushed mustard seeds and dijon-style French mustard.

nutmeg dried nut of an evergreen tree; available in ground form or you can grate your own with a fine grater.

oil

groundnut pressed from ground peanuts. The most commonly used oil in stir-frying because of its high smoke point.

olive mono-unsaturated; made from the pressing of tree-ripened olives. Extra virgin and virgin are the best, obtained from the first pressings of the olive, while extra light or light refers to the taste, not fat levels.

vegetable any number of oils sourced from plants rather than animal fats.

oregano has a woody stalk with clumps of tiny, dark green leaves that have a pungent, peppery flavour and are used fresh or dried.

papaya also known as pawpaw; large, pear-shaped red-orange tropical fruit. Sometimes used unripe (green) in cooking.

passionfruit also known as granadilla; a small tropical fruit, comprised of a tough dark-purple skin surrounding an edible pulp with black sweet-sour seeds.

pecans golden-brown, buttery and rich nuts. Good in savoury and sweet dishes.

peppercorns available in black, white, red or green.

pine nuts also known as pignoli; small, cream-coloured kernels obtained from the cones of different varieties of pine trees.

saffron one of the most expensive spices in the world, true saffron comes only from the saffron crocus.

shallots small, elongated, brown-skinned members of the onion family. Grows in tight clusters similar to garlic.

star anise a dried star-shaped pod, the seeds of which taste of aniseed.

sugar we used coarse, granulated table sugar, also known as crystal sugar, unless otherwise specified.

brown an extremely soft, fine granulated sugar retaining molasses for its deep colour and flavour.

caster also known as superfine or finely granulated table sugar.

palm made from the sap of the sugar palm tree. Light brown to black in colour; usually sold in rock-hard cakes. If unavailable, use brown sugar.

tamarind the tamarind tree produces clusters of hairy brown pods, each of which is filled with seeds and a viscous pulp, that are dried and pressed into blocks. Releases a sweet-sour, slightly astringent taste.

thyme a member of the mint family; has tiny grey-green leaves that give off a pungent minty, light-lemon aroma.

tomato

paste triple-concentrated tomato puree used to flavour soups, stews, sauces and casseroles.

sun-dried available loose (by weight) or in packets (not packed in oil).

treacle thick, dark syrup which is a by-product of sugar refining.

turmeric a member of the ginger family, its root is dried and ground; intensely pungent in taste but not hot.

vanilla pod dried long, thin pod from a tropical orchid; the tiny black seeds inside the bean are used to impart a distinctively sweet vanilla flavour.

vinegar

balsamic authentic only from the province of Modena, Italy; made from a regional wine of white trebbiano grapes specially processed then aged in antique wooden casks to give an exquisite pungent flavour.

cider made from fermented apples.

malt made from fermented malt and beech shavings.

red wine based on fermented red wine.

white made from spirit of cane sugar.

conversion charts

MEASURES

The cup and spoon measurements used in this book are metric: one measuring cup holds approximately 250ml; one metric tablespoon holds 20ml; one metric teaspoon holds 5ml.

All cup and spoon measurements are level.

The most accurate way of measuring dry ingredients is to weigh them. When measuring liquids, use a clear glass or plastic jug with metric markings.

We use large eggs with an average weight of 60g.

WARNING This book may contain recipes for dishes made with raw or lightly cooked eggs. These should be avoided by vulnerable people such as pregnant and nursing mothers, invalids, the elderly, babies and young children.

DRY MEASURES

METRIC	IMPERIAL
15g	½oz
30g	1oz
60g	2oz
90g	3oz
125g	4oz (¼lb)
155g	5oz
185g	6oz
220g	7oz
250g	8oz (½lb)
280g	9oz
315g	10oz
345g	11oz
375g	12oz (¾lb)
410g	13oz
440g	14oz
470g	15oz
500g	16oz (1lb)
750g	24oz (1½lb)
1kg	32oz (2lb)

LIQUID MEASURES

METRIC	IMPERIAL
30ml	1 fl oz
60ml	2 fl oz
100ml	3 fl oz
125ml	4 fl oz
150ml	5 fl oz (¼ pint/1 gill)
190ml	6 fl oz
250ml	8 fl oz
300ml	10 fl oz (½ pint)
500ml	16 fl oz
600ml	20 fl oz (1 pint)
1000ml (1 litre)	1¾ pints

LENGTH MEASURES

METRIC	IMPERIAL
3mm	⅛in
6mm	¼in
1cm	½in
2cm	¾in
2.5cm	1in
5cm	2in
6cm	2½in
8cm	3in
10cm	4in
13cm	5in
15cm	6in
18cm	7in
20cm	8in
23cm	9in
25cm	10in
28cm	11in
30cm	12in (1ft)

OVEN TEMPERATURES

These oven temperatures are only a guide for conventional ovens. For fan-assisted ovens, check the manufacturer's manual.

	°C (CELSIUS)	°F (FAHRENHEIT)	GAS MARK
Very low	120	250	½
Low	150	275–300	1–2
Moderately low	160	325	3
Moderate	180	350–375	4–5
Moderately hot	200	400	6
Hot	220	425–450	7–8
Very hot	240	475	9

index

This book is published by Octopus
Publishing Group Limited based
on materials licensed to it by
Bauer Media Books, Sydney
Bauer Media Books are published by
Bauer Media Limited
54 Park St, Sydney
GPO Box 4088, Sydney, NSW 2001.
phone (02) 9282 8618;
fax (02) 9126 3702
www.awwcookbooks.com.au

MEDIA GROUP
OCTOPUS BOOKS
Design: Chris Bell
Food Director: Pamela Clark

Published and Distributed in the
United Kingdom by Octopus Publishing
Group Limited
Endeavour House
189 Shaftesbury Avenue
London WC2H 8JY
United Kingdom
phone + 44 (0) 207 632 5400;
fax + 44 (0) 207 632 5405
aww@octopusbooks.co.uk;
www.octopusbooks.co.uk
www.australian-womens-weekly.com

To order books:
telephone LBS on 01903 828 503
order online at
www.australian-womens-weekly.com
or www.octopusbooks.co.uk

Printed and bound in Thailand

International foreign language rights,
Brian Cearnes, Bauer Media Books
bcearnes@bauer-media.com.au

A catalogue record for this book is
available from the British Library.
ISBN 978-1-90742-807-4
© Bauer Media Limited 2010
ABN 18 053 273 546
This publication is copyright.
No part of it may be reproduced or
transmitted in any form without the
written permission of the Publisher.
First published in 2010. Reprinted
2012, 2013.